deleted

D1223449

LET'S LEARN ABOUT LITERATURE

NONFICTION

Heather Moore Niver

Enslow Publishing
101 W. 23rd Street
Suite 240
New York, NY 10011
USA
enslow.com

Words to Know

autobiography The story of a person's life. It is written by that person.

biography The story of a person's life. It is written by another person.

fact A piece of information that is true.

fiction A story that is made up.

glossary The part of a book that gives the meaning of words.

index A list of subjects and the page numbers where they are found in a book.

nonfiction Writing based on facts.

oral Spoken out loud, not written.

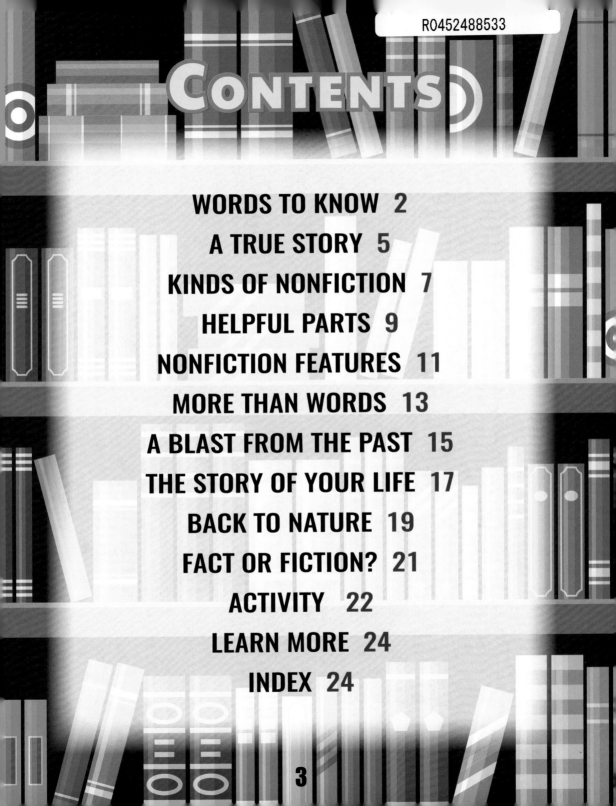

CONTENTS

Nonfiction books are full of interesting facts.

A True Story

Sometimes the best stories are true stories. These stories are called **nonfiction**. They are the opposite of **fiction**. Fiction is made up. Nonfiction gives you **facts**.

Nonfiction can teach us about events like the first moon landing.

Kinds of Nonfiction

Nonfiction can give us lots of information. It can be about real people or true events. Books about history or science are nonfiction.

FAST FACT

Other kinds of nonfiction include art, music, cooking, and sports.

TABLE OF CONTENTS.

———◆———

A table of contents tells us where to find the chapters in the book.

Helpful Parts

Many nonfiction books have a **glossary**. This tells us what words mean. There may also be an **index** at the end of a book. This is a list of subjects in the book. It has page numbers where readers can find information.

Fast Fact

The glossary and index are in alphabetical, or ABC, order.

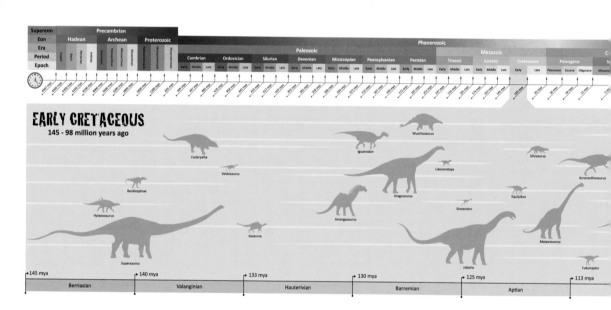

Supereon			Precambrian																																											
Eon	Hadean			Archean		Proterozoic																								Phanerozoic															
Era																				Paleozoic													Mesozoic										C
Period													Cambrian			Ordovician			Silurian			Devonian			Mississipian			Pennsylvanian			Permian			Triassic			Jurassic			Cretaceous		Paleogene			
Epoch													Early Middle Late			Early Middle Late			Early Middle Late			Early Middle Late			Early Middle Late			Early Middle Late			Early Middle Late			Early Middle Late			Early Late		Paleocene Eocene Oligocene			Miocene

EARLY CRETACEOUS
145 - 98 million years ago

Cedarpelta

Wuerhosaurus

Iguanodon

Silvisaurus

Valdosaurus

Liaoceratops

Acrocanthosaurus

Beckiespinax

Aragosaurus

Equijubus

Hylaeosaurus

Amargasaurus

Simenator

Gastonia

Malawisaurus

Supersaurus

Jobaria

Fukuiraptor

145 mya	140 mya	133 mya	130 mya	125 mya	113 mya
Berriasian	Valanginian	Hauterivian	Barremian	Aptian	

This timeline shows when different dinosaurs lived.

Nonfiction Features

In nonfiction, important words and ideas often stand out. Key words may be in **bold** or *italics*. An important idea may be in a text box—like the one on this page!

FAST FACT

In books about history, a timeline can show important dates and events.

PARTS OF A FLOWER

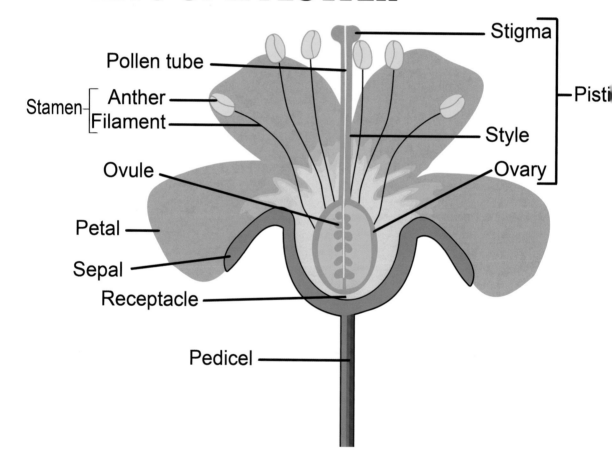

Stigma

Pollen tube

Pisti

Stamen — Anther
Filament

Style

Ovule

Ovary

Petal

Sepal

Receptacle

Pedicel

**Labels on a picture help
us to understand it better.**

More Than Words

Some nonfiction books include more than words. They may have photographs, pictures, or charts. These show important information. Sometimes they help explain difficult ideas.

A storyteller tells children about her family's history.

A Blast from the Past

History is a record of events from the past. A long time ago, histories were not written down. They were told **orally**. Stories were passed on from person to person.

Fast Fact

Sometimes oral histories were spoken as poetry.

Biographies are often written about important people like Benjamin Franklin.

The Story of Your Life

A **biography** tells the story of a person's life. One person writes the biography of another person. If you wrote your own life story, it would be called an **autobiography**.

FAST FACT

Now and Ben is a biography written about Benjamin Franklin and his inventions.

Some nonfiction books teach us how nature works.

Back to Nature

Nature writing is a popular type of nonfiction. It includes facts and information about the outside world. This can mean the plants and animals in your yard or the planets and stars in the sky!

FAST FACT

The Tiny Seed by Eric Carle is a nature book about a seed growing into a plant.

The real-life
Christopher Robin
with his toy bear

Fact or Fiction?

Sometimes nonfiction can be mixed with a little fiction. A book might be about real people and events. But some details, like conversations, may be made up.

FAST FACT

The children's book *Winnie the Bear* is based on the true story of the bear that inspired the Winnie-the-Pooh books by A. A. Milne.

Activity

Write Your Own Nonfiction

MATERIALS
- notebook
- pencil
- nonfiction books

Procedure:

It's easy to write your own work of nonfiction.

- Pick a subject you think is interesting, like an animal or an event in history.
- Go to the library and find at

least three nonfiction books about your topic. You could also use three websites. Have your parent, guardian, or teacher help.

- Write down ten interesting facts about your topic.
- Show your choices to an adult. They can help make sure your information is correct.
- Now use your own words to explain your facts.
- You can include photos, too.
- Try writing a table of contents or a glossary!

Books

Nagle, Jeanne. *What Is Nonfiction?* New York, NY: Britannica Educational Publishing, 2015.

100 Events That Made History. New York, NY: DK Publishing, 2016.

Osborne, Mary Pope. *Magic Tree House Incredible Fact Book*. New York, NY: Random House, 2016.

Websites

Fiction vs. Nonfiction Jeopardy
www.quia.com/cb/258031.html
Test your skills! Can you guess which is fiction and which is nonfiction?

Kids Are Writers: Nonfiction
kidsarewriters.com/category/non-fiction/
Get some great ideas for writing your own nonfiction.

INDEX

Published in 2019 by Enslow Publishing, LLC.
101 W. 23rd Street, Suite 240, New York, NY 10011

Copyright © 2019 by Enslow Publishing, LLC.

Library of Congress Cataloging-in-Publication Data

Names: Niver, Heather Moore, author.
Title: Nonfiction / Heather Moore Niver.
Description: New York, NY : Enslow Publishing, LLC., [2019] | Series: Let's learn about literature | Audience: Grades K-4 |Includes bibliographical references and index.
Identifiers: LCCN 2017045162| ISBN 9780766096028 (library bound) | ISBN 9780766096042 (paperback) | ISBN 9780766096059 (6 pack)
Subjects: LCSH: Literature—Study and teaching (Elementary) | Literary form—Study and teaching (Elementary) | Language arts (Elementary)
Classification: LCC PN3427 .N585 2019 | DDC 808/.036—dc23
LC record available at https://lccn.loc.gov/2017045162

Printed in the United States of America

Photo Credits: Cover, p. 1 Africa Studio/Shutterstock.com; pp. 2-3, 24 Gurza/Shutterstock.com; p. 4 Akiko Aoki/Moment/Getty Images; pp. 5, 7, 9, 11, 13, 15, 17, 19, 21, 22-23 (paper, notebook, pencil) narmacero/Shutterstock.com; pp. 5, 7, 11, 15, 17, 19, 21, 22 (open book) Wen Wen/Shutterstock.com; p. 6 Bettmann/Getty Images; p. 8 Paul Fearn/Alamy Stock Photo; p. 10 Nerdist72/Shutterstock.com; p. 12 ducu59us/Shutterstock.com; p. 14 Photo Researchers/Science Source/Getty Images; p. 16 Everett Art/Shutterstock.com; p. 18 Singkham/Shutterstock.com; p. 20 Pictorial Press Ltd/Alamy Stock Photo; p. 22 stoatphoto/Shutterstock.com.